MW01244294

RIDE THROUGH TIME

A History of Motorcycles

Zackary B. Wright

Steven R. Buchko

Copyright © 2023 Zackary B. Wright

All rights reserved

The characters and events portrayed in this book are fictitious. Any similarity to real persons, living or dead, is coincidental and not intended by the author.

No part of this book may be reproduced, or stored in a retrieval system, or transmitted in any form or by any means, electronic, mechanical, photocopying, recording, or otherwise, without express written permission of the publisher.

ISBN: 9798385567157
Imprint: Independently published

Library of Congress Control Number: 2018675309
Printed in the United States of America

This book is dedicated to all future riders, who will carry on the legacy and passion of motorcycles for generations to come.

May you always feel the wind in your face and the thrill of the ride, and may the spirit of adventure and individualism that has always defined motorcycles continue to inspire you throughout your journey.

Remember to ride with respect for yourself, others, and the environment, and to always be safe and responsible on two wheels.

To all future riders, this book is for you.

CONTENTS

RIDE THROUGH TIME: A HISTORY OF MOTORCYCLES

By Zackary B. Wright

CHAPTER 1: ORIGINS OF THE MOTORCYCLE

The history of the motorcycle is a rich tapestry woven from the threads of human innovation and ingenuity. From the earliest designs and experiments in motorized transportation, to the development of the internal combustion engine, the introduction of the safety bicycle, and the birth of the first motorcycles and their manufacturers, the story of the motorcycle is one of great intrigue and fascination.

Early Designs and Experiments in Motorized Transportation

The early experiments in motorized transportation were driven by a desire to find faster and more efficient means of travel. One of the earliest and most notable attempts at

developing a steam-powered vehicle was made by Nicolas-Joseph Cugnot in 1769. His invention, a steam-powered tricycle, had limited success due to its heavy weight and lack of reliability.

However, Cugnot's invention set the stage for further development in the field of motorized transportation. In the 1830s, Robert Anderson developed an electric carriage, which was powered by a battery and had a top speed of around 4 mph.

Development of the Internal Combustion Engine

The internal combustion engine, which powers most modern motorcycles, was first developed in the mid-19th century. In 1860, French engineer Etienne Lenoir developed the first practical internal combustion engine, which ran on a mixture of coal gas and air. The engine was first used to power a boat, but Lenoir soon realized its potential for use in other forms of transportation.

Over the next few decades, the internal combustion engine continued to evolve, with numerous inventors making important contributions to its development. In 1876, Nikolaus Otto invented the four-stroke engine, which is still used in most cars and motorcycles today. This new engine was much more efficient than Lenoir's engine, producing more power with less fuel.

Introduction of the Safety Bicycle and Its Influence

on Motorcycle Design

In the late 19th century, the safety bicycle was introduced, featuring a diamond-shaped frame, two wheels of equal size, and a chain drive. This new design was much safer and more stable than earlier designs, and quickly became popular with cyclists.

The safety bicycle also had a significant impact on motorcycle design. Motorcycle manufacturers began to incorporate elements of the safety bicycle into their designs, such as the diamond-shaped frame, the chain drive, and the pneumatic tire. These innovations made motorcycles more stable and easier to ride, and paved the way for the development of more powerful and sophisticated machines.

First Motorcycles and Their Manufacturers

The first true motorcycles appeared in the late 19th century, and were essentially bicycles with small, gasoline-powered engines attached. One of the earliest of these machines was the Daimler Reitwagen, which was built in 1885 by Gottlieb Daimler and Wilhelm Maybach. The Reitwagen had a wooden frame, two wheels of equal size, and a small gasoline engine mounted on the frame.

Other manufacturers soon followed suit, and by the turn of the century, motorcycles were being produced by companies such as Indian, Harley-

Davidson, and Triumph. These early motorcycles were simple machines, with single-cylinder engines and belt or chain drives. They were often used for racing or as an alternative to the horse-drawn carriage.

Conclusion

The history of the motorcycle is a fascinating and complex one, with numerous inventors and innovators contributing to its development over the centuries. From the earliest steam-powered vehicles to the modern, high-performance machines of today, the motorcycle has come a long way. Its origins can be traced back to the early experiments in motorized transportation, the development of the internal combustion engine, the introduction of the safety bicycle, and the birth of the first motorcycles and their manufacturers. These early milestones set the stage for the motorcycle's evolution as a mode of transportation, recreation, and sport. Over time, motorcycles have become an integral part of popular culture, inspiring a sense of freedom, adventure, and rebellion.

As we have seen, the history of the motorcycle is a complex and fascinating one, shaped by the ingenuity and creativity of countless inventors, engineers, and designers. In the following chapters, we will explore the milestones, people, and events that have shaped the motorcycle's

evolution and contributed to its enduring appeal. We will delve into the history of motorcycle racing, the emergence of motorcycle culture, and the technological advancements that continue to drive the industry forward. Join us on this journey through time, as we ride through the history of motorcycles.

CHAPTER 2: RACING IN THE EARLY YEARS

Motorcycle racing has been an integral part of the motorcycle's history since its inception. In this chapter, we will explore the early years of motorcycle racing, including the first motorcycle races and competitions, notable riders and their achievements, and the growth of motorcycle racing as a sport. We will also delve into some epic, but long-forgotten races that have helped shape the sport into what it is today.

First Motorcycle Races and Competitions

The first motorcycle race on record took place in 1894 in France, with a distance of around 1.2 km. The race was won by Jules Truffault, who rode a petrol-powered De Dion-Bouton tricycle. This race was quickly followed by other events across Europe, including Germany, Italy, and the United Kingdom.

In 1903, the Federation Internationale de Motocyclisme (FIM) was established to oversee international motorcycle racing, and by 1907, the Isle of Man Tourist Trophy (TT) had been founded, which would go on to become one of the most prestigious motorcycle races in the world.

Notable Riders and Their Achievements

In the early years of motorcycle racing, there were several notable riders who made significant contributions to the sport. One of the most famous was Charles Franklin, who rode for the Indian motorcycle company. Franklin won several races throughout the 1910s and 1920s, including the Isle of Man TT in 1920.

Another notable rider was Jimmie Guthrie, who won the Isle of Man TT three times between 1930 and 1937. Guthrie was known for his aggressive riding style and his skill at racing on both the road and the track.

Growth of Motorcycle Racing as a Sport

Throughout the early 20th century, motorcycle racing continued to grow in popularity, with increased events being organized across the world. In the 1930s, the sport underwent a major transformation, with the introduction of more powerful machines and the development of new racing techniques.

During this time, motorcycle racing became more

professionalized, with riders signing contracts with manufacturers and competing in events for prize money. The Isle of Man TT continued to be one of the most prestigious events in the sport, but new races, such as the Grand Prix races in Europe, also began to emerge.

Epic, but Long-Forgotten Races

While the Isle of Man TT and other well-known races remain important events in the history of motorcycle racing, there are several epic, but long-forgotten races that deserve recognition. One such race was the International Six Days Trial, which was first held in 1913 in Carlisle, England. This event was a grueling test of endurance, with riders covering up to 1,000 miles over six days on difficult terrain.

Another forgotten race was the Australian TT, which was held in Bathurst, New South Wales between 1913 and 1921. This event was notable for its challenging track, which included a steep hill climb and a section of cobblestones.

Conclusion

The early years of motorcycle racing were marked by the emergence of new events and the rise of notable riders who helped shape the sport into what it is today. From the first motorcycle races in the late 19th century to the growth of the sport in the early 20th century, motorcycle

racing has undergone significant changes over the years. While some races have been forgotten, they remain an important part of the sport's history, and their legacy lives on through the events and riders of today.

CHAPTER 3: MOTORCYCLES IN WORLD WAR I AND II

Motorcycles played a crucial role in both World War I and World War II. In this chapter, we will explore the military use of motorcycles during these wars, the technological advancements made during the conflicts, and the influence they had on post-war motorcycle design. We will also delve into some of the secrets of the war involving motorcycles, including little-known facts that shed new light on their use and impact.

Military Use of Motorcycles

During World War I, motorcycles were used primarily for reconnaissance and messenger duties. They were often fitted with machine guns and other weapons and used in combat situations. The lightweight and maneuverable nature of motorcycles made them ideal for use in the trenches and on rough terrain, allowing soldiers to quickly move messages and supplies across the battlefield.

In World War II, motorcycles continued to be used for reconnaissance and messenger duties, as well as for transporting troops and equipment. One notable example was the use of the BMW R75 motorcycle by German troops in the North African campaign. The R75 was a versatile machine that could be fitted with a sidecar or a mounted machine gun, and was used to great effect by German forces in desert warfare.

Technological Advancements During the Wars

The use of motorcycles in World War I and World War II led to numerous technological advancements. During World War I, motorcycles were fitted with radios, enabling soldiers to communicate more effectively on the battlefield. In World War II, motorcycles were equipped with advanced navigation systems, including compasses and GPS devices, which allowed troops to navigate through unfamiliar terrain.

The wars also saw the development of new types of motorcycles, such as the Indian 841, which was designed specifically for military use. The 841 was a high-performance machine that could reach speeds of up to 90 mph and was used by American forces in both World War I and World War II.

Influence on Post-War Motorcycle Design

The use of motorcycles in World War I and World War II had a significant influence on post-war motorcycle design. Military motorcycles were often built to withstand harsh conditions and rough terrain, and were designed to be lightweight and maneuverable. These features were incorporated into post-war motorcycles, such as the Harley-Davidson Servi-Car, which was designed for use by police and other law enforcement agencies.

The wars also led to the development of new technologies that were later incorporated into civilian motorcycles. For example, the use of hydraulic brakes, which were first developed for military motorcycles, eventually became standard on most motorcycles.

Secrets of the War Involving Motorcycles

The use of motorcycles in World War I and World War II also led to a number of secrets and little-known facts that shed new light on the conflicts. One example is the use of Indian motorcycles by the US Army in World War I, which were painted in camouflage to blend in with the surrounding environment.

Another little-known fact is the use of motorcycles by British forces to transport pigeons, which were used to carry messages between troops.

The motorcycles would transport the pigeons to a central location, where they would be released to fly back to their home base with important messages.

Conclusion

The use of motorcycles in World War I and World War II had a significant impact on the conflicts and on the development of motorcycles as a whole. From their use in reconnaissance and messenger duties, to the development of new technologies and designs, motorcycles played a vital role in the wars. The secrets and little-known facts surrounding their use add a fascinating dimension to their history and continue to shed new light on their impact.

CHAPTER 3: MOTORCYCLES IN WORLD WAR I AND II

Motorcycles played a crucial role in both World War I and World War II. In this chapter, we will explore the military use of motorcycles during these wars, the technological advancements made during the conflicts, and the influence they had on post-war motorcycle design. We will also delve into some of the secrets of the war involving motorcycles, including little-known facts that shed new light on their use and impact.

Military Use of Motorcycles

During World War I, motorcycles were used primarily for reconnaissance and messenger duties. They were often fitted with machine guns and other weapons and used in combat situations. The lightweight and maneuverable nature of motorcycles made them ideal for use in the trenches and on rough terrain, allowing soldiers to quickly move messages and supplies across the battlefield.

In World War II, motorcycles continued to be used for reconnaissance and messenger duties, as well as for transporting troops and equipment. One notable example was the use of the BMW R75 motorcycle by German troops in the North African campaign. The R75 was a versatile machine that could be fitted with a sidecar or a mounted machine gun, and was used to great effect by German forces in desert warfare.

Technological Advancements During the Wars

The use of motorcycles in World War I and World War II led to numerous technological advancements. During World War I, motorcycles were fitted with radios, enabling soldiers to communicate more effectively on the battlefield. In World War II, motorcycles were equipped with advanced navigation systems, including compasses and GPS devices, which allowed troops to navigate through unfamiliar terrain.

The wars also saw the development of new types of motorcycles, such as the Indian 841, which was designed specifically for military use. The 841 was a high-performance machine that could reach speeds of up to 90 mph and was used by American forces in both World War I and World War II.

Influence on Post-War Motorcycle Design

The use of motorcycles in World War I and World War II had a significant influence on post-war motorcycle design. Military motorcycles were often built to withstand harsh conditions and rough terrain, and were designed to be lightweight and maneuverable. These features were incorporated into post-war motorcycles, such as the Harley-Davidson Servi-Car, which was designed for use by police and other law enforcement agencies.

The wars also led to the development of new technologies that were later incorporated into civilian motorcycles. For example, the use of hydraulic brakes, which were first developed for military motorcycles, eventually became standard on most motorcycles.

Secrets of the War Involving Motorcycles

The use of motorcycles in World War I and World War II also led to a number of secrets and little-known facts that shed new light on the conflicts. One example is the use of Indian motorcycles by the US Army in World War I, which were painted in camouflage to blend in with the surrounding environment.

Another little-known fact is the use of motorcycles by British forces to transport pigeons, which were used to carry messages between troops.

The motorcycles would transport the pigeons to a central location, where they would be released to fly back to their home base with important messages.

Conclusion

The use of motorcycles in World War I and World War II had a significant impact on the conflicts and on the development of motorcycles as a whole. From their use in reconnaissance and messenger duties, to the development of new technologies and designs, motorcycles played a vital role in the wars. The secrets and little-known facts surrounding their use add a fascinating dimension to their history and continue to shed new light on their impact.

CHAPTER 4: ISLE OF MAN TT

The Isle of Man TT is one of the most iconic motorcycle races in the world, with a rich history dating back over 100 years. In this chapter, we will explore the origins of the race, the evolution of the course and its challenges, and the notable races and riders in Isle of Man history. We will also delve into some unique and lesser-known facts about the race, including its brutal nature, the number of fatalities, and the sheer scale of the event.

Origins of the Race

The Isle of Man TT was first held in 1907, with riders competing on a 15-mile course through the winding roads of the Isle of Man. The race quickly gained a reputation for being one of the most challenging and dangerous events in motorcycle racing, with riders reaching speeds of up to 60 mph on roads that were not designed for racing.

Over the years, the race has undergone many

changes, with the course being extended and modified to make it even more challenging. Today, the Isle of Man TT is considered one of the ultimate tests of motorcycle racing skill and endurance.

Evolution of the Course and Its Challenges

The course for the Isle of Man TT has undergone numerous changes since the race's start. In 1911, the course was extended to 37.75 miles, and in 1920, the famous "Mountain Course" was introduced, which included a climb up Snaefell Mountain.

The Mountain Course is considered one of the most challenging race courses in the world, with 200 corners, narrow roads, and steep inclines. The course is also known for its many jumps and bumps, which can be extremely dangerous at high speeds.

Notable Races and Riders in Isle of Man History

The Isle of Man TT has been home to many notable races and riders over the years. One of the most famous races in TT history was the 1967 Senior TT, which saw Mike Hailwood come out of retirement to win the race on a four-cylinder Honda.

Other notable riders in Isle of Man history include Giacomo Agostini, who won 10 TT races between 1965 and 1972, and Joey Dunlop, who won a record-breaking 26 TT races before his tragic death in 2000.

Fatality Statistics

Despite the Isle of Man TT being a beloved and iconic race, the event has had a high number of fatalities throughout its history. Since the event began in 1907, there have been 259 rider fatalities. This high number is due in part to the challenging nature of the course, the speeds at which riders travel, and the fact that the roads are not closed off during the event.

While many safety measures have been implemented over the years, including improved protective gear for riders, stricter regulations on bike specifications, and increased medical support, the danger of the race remains a significant concern.

Unique Facts About the Race

In addition to the high number of fatalities and the challenge of the course, there are many unique facts about the Isle of Man TT that add to its intrigue. For example, the race is not held every year, but instead takes place biannually, with races being held in even-numbered years. This is due to the high costs of organizing the event and the need for the island to recover between races.

Another unique aspect of the race is the sheer scale of the event. The Isle of Man TT attracts tens of thousands of spectators from around the world, making it one of the largest motorsports events in the world. The event also generates a significant amount of revenue for the island, with estimates suggesting that it contributes over £30 million to the local economy.

In conclusion, the Isle of Man TT is a race that has captured the hearts and minds of motorcycle racing fans around the world for over a century. Its challenging course, notable races and riders, and unique history have all contributed to its status as one of the most iconic motorsports events in the world.

However, the race is also known for its high number of fatalities, which highlights the extreme danger that riders face when competing. Despite this, the Isle of Man TT remains an important and beloved event for many people, and its unique aspects, such as the biannual schedule and the huge number of spectators, only add to its allure.

As the race continues to evolve and adapt to changing times, it remains a testament to the skill, endurance, and courage of the riders who take on its challenges. The Isle of Man TT will undoubtedly continue to captivate audiences and push riders to their limits for years to come.

CHAPTER 5: RISE OF THE AMERICAN MOTORCYCLE INDUSTRY

The American motorcycle industry has a rich history that spans over a century, and has been dominated by two iconic brands: Harley-Davidson and Indian motorcycles. In this chapter, we will explore the origins of these two brands, the motorcycle culture that developed in America, and the notable events and races that have shaped the industry. We will also delve into some unique and lesser-known facts about the American motorcycle industry that shed light on its enduring appeal.

Harley-Davidson and Indian Motorcycles

Harley-Davidson and Indian motorcycles are two

of the most iconic brands in the history of motorcycling. Both companies have a long and storied history, with Harley-Davidson being founded in 1903 in Milwaukee, Wisconsin, and Indian motorcycles being founded in 1901 in Springfield, Massachusetts.

Over the years, both companies have faced their fair share of challenges, including financial struggles, competition from other manufacturers, and changing consumer preferences. However, both brands have endured and continue to produce some of the most sought-after motorcycles in the world.

Motorcycle Culture in America

The American motorcycle culture has been shaped by many different factors, including movies, music, and the open road. The motorcycle has long been associated with freedom, rebellion, and individualism, and has played a significant role in popular culture.

One of the most notable aspects of the American motorcycle culture is the "biker" subculture, which has its roots in the 1940s and 1950s. Bikers are often associated with leather jackets, long hair, and a love of rock music. However, the biker subculture has also been linked to criminal activity and gang violence, which has led to a negative perception of bikers in some circles.

Notable American Motorcycle Events and Races

The American motorcycle industry has been home to many notable events and races over the years. One of the most famous is the Sturgis Motorcycle Rally, which is held every year in Sturgis, South Dakota. The rally attracts hundreds of thousands of visitors from around the world and is one of the largest motorcycle events in the world.

Another notable event is the Daytona Bike Week, which is held every year in Daytona Beach, Florida. The event features a wide range of activities, including motorcycle races, bike shows, and live music.

The American motorcycle industry has also been home to many notable races, including the famous Daytona 200, which has been held since 1937. The race is considered one of the most prestigious events in American motorcycle racing and has been won by many of the sport's most famous riders.

Unique Facts About the American Motorcycle Industry

Despite the popularity and enduring appeal of the American motorcycle industry, there are many unique and lesser-known facts that shed light on its history and impact. For example, did you know that Harley-Davidson was the largest motorcycle manufacturer in the world during World War II, producing more than 90,000 motorcycles for the US military?

Another little-known fact is that the iconic Indian motorcycle brand was actually revived in 1999 by a group of investors who bought the rights to the name. The new Indian motorcycles have been praised for their classic design and high-quality craftsmanship.

In conclusion, the history of motorcycles is a fascinating journey that spans over a century and has been shaped by countless innovations, iconic brands, and notable events. From the origins of the motorcycle and the development of the internal combustion engine to the rise of the American motorcycle industry and the challenges and triumphs of motorcycle racing, the story of motorcycles is one of perseverance, passion, and creativity.

Throughout this book, we have explored the early designs and experiments in motorized transportation, the development of the internal combustion engine, and the introduction of the safety bicycle and its influence on motorcycle design. We have also delved into the origins of motorcycle racing, the growth of the sport, and the notable riders and races that have made their mark on history. Additionally, we have examined the role of motorcycles in World War I and II, their military use, technological advancements, and the

influence on post-war motorcycle design.

One of the most iconic events in motorcycle racing is the Isle of Man TT, which has a rich history dating back over 100 years. The race's challenging course, notable races and riders, and unique history have all contributed to its status as one of the most iconic motorsports events in the world. Similarly, the American motorcycle industry has a rich history that spans over a century and has been dominated by two iconic brands, Harley-Davidson and Indian motorcycles. The industry has been shaped by many different factors, including movies, music, and the open road, and has played a significant role in popular culture.

Despite the challenges faced by the motorcycle industry over the years, it has continued to evolve and adapt to changing times. Manufacturers have introduced new technologies, materials, and designs that have improved the performance, safety, and comfort of motorcycles. Similarly, motorcycle racing has evolved to become a more organized, regulated, and safe sport, while still maintaining its excitement and allure.

As we come to the end of this book, it is clear that the history of motorcycles is a never-ending story of innovation, creativity, and perseverance. Its impact on popular culture and society is undeniable, and its enduring appeal shows no signs of fading. The motorcycle remains a symbol

of freedom, adventure, and individualism, and will undoubtedly continue to captivate and inspire people for generations to come.

CHAPTER 6: GOLDEN AGE OF MOTORCYCLE RACING

The 1950s and 1960s are widely regarded as the golden age of motorcycle racing, a time when the sport reached its peak of its popularity and witnessed the introduction of new technologies and design advancements that defined the era. In this chapter, we will explore the iconic races and riders that emerged during this time and delve into the technological advancements that made the golden age of motorcycle racing so special.

Peak of Popularity

The 1950s and 1960s were a time of great growth and popularity for motorcycle racing. The sport had reached a wider audience and had become a significant part of popular culture. The rise in popularity can be attributed to a number of factors, including the growth of television and media coverage, the emergence of new technologies, and the introduction of new race circuits.

Iconic Races and Riders

The golden age of motorcycle racing was defined by some of the most iconic races and riders in the sport's history. One of the most famous races during this time was the Isle of Man TT, which continued to attract some of the best riders in the world. The TT witnessed some of the most thrilling races in motorcycle racing history, with riders reaching incredible speeds on the winding roads of the Isle of Man.

The golden age of motorcycle racing also witnessed the emergence of some of the most legendary riders in the sport's history. One of the most famous was John Surtees, who won the world championship on both two and four wheels, a feat that has never been repeated. Other notable riders from this era include Mike Hailwood, Phil Read, and Giacomo Agostini, who all achieved great success on the world stage.

Technological Advancements and Design Innovations

The golden age of motorcycle racing was also marked by a number of technological advancements and design innovations that transformed the sport. One of the most significant innovations was the introduction of disc brakes, which allowed riders to brake more effectively and safely at high speeds.

Another important innovation was the introduction of two-stroke engines, which were lighter and more powerful than their four-stroke counterparts. The development of the two-stroke engine revolutionized the sport and paved the way for the modern high-performance motorcycles that we see today.

The golden age of motorcycle racing also witnessed the introduction of new materials, such as magnesium and titanium, which allowed for lighter and stronger frames and components. This, in turn, led to greater speed and agility on the race track.

Conclusion

The golden age of motorcycle racing was a time of great growth, popularity, and innovation for the sport. The emergence of new technologies and design advancements transformed the sport, and the iconic races and riders that appeared during this time continue to inspire and captivate audiences to this day.

The golden age of motorcycle racing represented a time of great achievement, with riders pushing the limits of what was possible on two wheels. It was a time when the sport was at its peak of popularity, and its impact on popular culture and society cannot be overstated.

As we look back on this era, it is clear that the golden age of motorcycle racing will always hold a special place in the hearts and minds of racing fans around the world. Its legacy continues to inspire new generations of riders and racers, and its enduring appeal shows no signs of fading.

CHAPTER 7: FAMOUS MOTORCYCLES AND RIDERS

The world of motorcycles has produced some of the most iconic and legendary riders and motorcycles in history. In this chapter, we will explore the legends of the sport and their iconic motorcycles, riders who have made significant contributions to the sport, and the notable motorcycles that have left an indelible mark on motorcycle history.

Legends of the Sport and Their Iconic Motorcycles

There have been many legendary riders who have made significant contributions to the sport and left their mark on motorcycle history. Some of the most iconic riders include Valentino Rossi, who has won multiple world championships and is widely regarded as one of the greatest motorcycle racers of all time. Other notable riders include

Wayne Rainey, Kenny Roberts, and Mike Hailwood, who all achieved great success on the world stage.

The motorcycles that these riders rode have also become iconic symbols of the sport. One of the most famous motorcycles is the Yamaha YZR-M1, which has been ridden by Valentino Rossi to multiple world championships. Other famous motorcycles include the Honda RC211V, the Suzuki GSX-R750, and the Ducati Desmosedici GP.

Riders Who Have Made Significant Contributions to the Sport

In addition to the legendary riders, there are also many riders who have made significant contributions to the sport in other ways. For example, Kevin Cameron is a renowned motorcycle journalist and author who has written extensively on motorcycle technology and design. He has also served as the technical editor for Cycle World magazine for over 30 years.

Another notable rider is Keith Code, who is a former racer and founder of the California Superbike School. The school is one of the most prestigious motorcycle training programs in the world and has trained thousands of riders over the years.

Notable Motorcycles and Their Place in Motorcycle History

There are many motorcycles that have left an

indelible mark on motorcycle history, either because of their innovative design, technological advancements, or their impact on popular culture. One of the most famous motorcycles is the Harley-Davidson Knucklehead, which was introduced in 1936 and helped to establish Harley-Davidson as one of the most iconic motorcycle brands in the world.

Another famous motorcycle is the Honda CB750, which was introduced in 1969 and is widely regarded as the first "superbike." The CB750 helped to establish Honda as a major player in the motorcycle industry and was the first motorcycle to feature a transverse, four-cylinder engine.

Other notable motorcycles include the Triumph Bonneville, the Kawasaki Z1, and the BMW R80GS, which helped to establish the adventure touring category of motorcycles.

Conclusion

The world of motorcycles has produced some of the most iconic and legendary riders and motorcycles in history. From the legendary riders and their iconic motorcycles to the notable motorcycles that have left an indelible mark on motorcycle history, the sport has a rich and storied past.

The impact of these legendary riders and iconic motorcycles is still felt today and continues

to inspire new generations of riders and racers. The motorcycle remains a symbol of freedom, adventure, and individualism, and will undoubtedly continue to captivate and inspire people for generations to come.

CHAPTER 9: MOTORCYCLE RACING TODAY

Motorcycle racing is a global sport with a rich and storied history, but what is the current state of motorcycle racing? In this chapter, we will explore the current state of motorcycle racing, notable modern events and competitions, and emerging trends and technologies in motorcycle design.

Current State of Motorcycle Racing

Motorcycle racing continues to be a popular and exciting sport, with millions of fans around the world. Some of the most popular motorcycle racing events include MotoGP, World Superbike, and the Isle of Man TT. These events attract the best riders from around the world and offer some of the most thrilling races in motorcycle racing history.

One of the challenges facing motorcycle racing today is the increasing cost of competing at the highest level. The cost of developing and maintaining a competitive motorcycle team can run into the millions of dollars, which makes it difficult for smaller teams to compete with the larger, more established teams.

Notable Modern Events and Competitions

There are many notable modern events and competitions in motorcycle racing, including MotoGP, World Superbike, and the Suzuka 8 Hours endurance race. These events attract the best riders from around the world and offer some of the most thrilling races in motorcycle racing history.

Another notable event is the Dakar Rally, which is an off-road endurance race that takes place in South America. The race covers thousands of kilometers over some of the toughest terrain in the world and is a true test of skill and endurance for both the riders and their machines.

Emerging Trends and Technologies in Motorcycle Design

Motorcycle design is constantly evolving, with new technologies and materials being developed all the time. One of the most significant emerging trends in motorcycle design is the use of electric power. Electric motorcycles are becoming increasingly popular, and some manufacturers are even starting to produce electric racing motorcycles.

Another emerging trend is the use of advanced

materials such as carbon fiber and titanium, which allow for lighter and stronger frames and components. These materials are also being used to develop new aerodynamic designs that improve the speed and handling of motorcycles.

Conclusion

Motorcycle racing continues to be a popular and exciting sport with a bright future ahead. The current state of motorcycle racing is characterized by the increasing cost of competing at the highest level, but this has not diminished the enthusiasm and passion of fans around the world.

There are many notable modern events and competitions in motorcycle racing, and emerging trends and technologies in motorcycle design continue to push the boundaries of what is possible on two wheels. As we look ahead to the future of motorcycle racing, we can be sure that the sport will continue to evolve and captivate audiences around the world.

CHAPTER 10: FUTURE OF MOTORCYCLES

The world of motorcycles is constantly evolving, with new technologies and design innovations being developed all the time. In this chapter, we will explore the potential directions for motorcycle design and technology, environmental considerations and the future of the industry, as well as the challenges and opportunities facing the motorcycle industry in the coming years.

Potential Directions for Motorcycle Design and Technology

The future of motorcycle design and technology is exciting and full of possibilities. One potential direction is the continued development of electric motorcycles, which offer a cleaner and more sustainable alternative to traditional gasoline-powered motorcycles.

Another potential direction is the use of

advanced materials and technologies to improve the performance and safety of motorcycles. For example, the use of sensors and advanced computer systems could help to prevent accidents by alerting riders to potential hazards.

There is also the potential for the development of autonomous motorcycles, which could help to reduce accidents by removing the potential for human error. These motorcycles could also offer new opportunities for transportation and mobility, particularly in densely populated urban areas.

Environmental Considerations and the Future of the Industry

Environmental considerations are increasingly important in the motorcycle industry, and manufacturers are looking for ways to reduce the carbon footprint of their products. Electric motorcycles are one solution, but there are also other ways to reduce the environmental impact of motorcycles.

For example, the use of lighter and more efficient materials could help to reduce the energy needed to manufacture and transport motorcycles. Additionally, the development of more fuel-efficient engines could help to reduce the environmental impact of gasoline-powered motorcycles.

Challenges and Opportunities Facing the Motorcycle Industry

The motorcycle industry is facing a number of challenges and opportunities in the coming years. One of the biggest challenges is the increasing regulation of motorcycles, particularly in regard to emissions and safety standards.

However, there are also many opportunities for the motorcycle industry, particularly in emerging markets such as Asia and Africa. These markets offer significant growth potential for manufacturers, and there is also the potential for the development of new and innovative products that are tailored to the unique needs and preferences of these markets.

Prediction for the Future of Motorcycles

The future of motorcycles is bright and full of possibilities. In the coming years, we can expect to see continued development of electric motorcycles, as well as the use of advanced materials and technologies to improve the performance and safety of motorcycles.

There is also the potential for the development of autonomous motorcycles, which could revolutionize the way we think about transportation and mobility. As environmental considerations become increasingly important, we can expect to see a continued focus on the

development of more sustainable and eco-friendly motorcycles.

Overall, the future of motorcycles is exciting and full of potential. As the industry continues to evolve and innovate, we can expect to see new and exciting products that push the boundaries of what is possible on two wheels.

Thank you for joining me on this journey through the history and future of motorcycles. As a lifelong fan of racing and fast machines, I have always been fascinated by the world of motorcycles and the incredible feats of speed and skill that are possible on two wheels.

In writing this book, my goal was to share my passion for motorcycles and their rich and varied history with readers around the world. From the early designs and experiments in motorized transportation to the emerging trends and technologies of the future, I have tried to capture the spirit and excitement of this incredible sport.

I hope that this book has inspired you to learn more about motorcycles and their place in the world of racing and beyond. Whether you are a seasoned rider or simply a fan of fast machines and thrilling competition, the world of motorcycles is one that will continue to captivate and inspire for years to come.

Thank you for reading, and I hope to see you at the racetrack soon.

-Zackary B. Wright

ABOUT THE AUTHOR

Zackary B. Wright

Zackary B. Wright is a writer and avid fan of competitive sports, particularly racing. Born and raised in Wyandotte, Michigan, Zackary has always had a passion for anything that involves engines, adrenaline, and going fast.

When he's not writing, Zackary can often be found at the racetrack, watching his favorite drivers and teams compete. He has a deep knowledge of racing engines and loves nothing more than the thrill of watching a race unfold.

Zackary's love for racing and fast machines inspired him to write this book, which explores the rich history and exciting future of motorcycles. He hopes that readers will share his passion for this incredible sport and come away with a deeper appreciation for the machines, riders, and events that make it all possible.

Made in the USA
Middletown, DE
11 March 2023